# As Is

# As Is

## JAMES GALVIN

COPPER CANYON PRESS
PORT TOWNSEND, WASHINGTON

Printed in the United States of America

Cover art: Robert and Shana ParkeHarrison, "Overflow," 2006. Mixed media and archival print on dibond, 30 x 46 inches.

Copper Canyon Press is in residence at Fort Worden State Park in Port Townsend, Washington, under the auspices of Centrum. Centrum is a gathering place for artists and creative thinkers from around the world, students of all ages and backgrounds, and audiences seeking extraordinary cultural enrichment.

Thanks to the magazines in which some of these poems first appeared: *American Poet, Caffeine Destiny, Carnet de Route, Colorado Review, Guernica, Matter, Orion, Smartish Pace, The Threepenny Review, Tin House, Verse, Volt,* and *The Yale Review.*

"No Bastion" was anthologized in *The Wide Open,* and "Girl without Her Nightgown" was included in *The Best American Poetry 2008.*

LIBRARY OF CONGRESS CATALOGING-IN-PUBLICATION DATA
Galvin, James.
  As is / by James Galvin.
    p. cm.
  Poems.
  ISBN 978-1-55659-296-6 (alk. paper)
  I. Title.

PS3557.A444A9 2009
811'.54—dc22

                                        2008049369

98765432 first printing

COPPER CANYON PRESS
Post Office Box 271
Port Townsend, Washington 98368
www.coppercanyonpress.org

FOR DORA

# CONTENTS

# As Is

# A Tiny yet Nonexistent Etching as Seen through a Magnifying Glass

*after Rembrandt*

Everything is drawn
With excruciating precision:
The grape arbor sheltering the children
Who are playing with a pig bladder,
The thatched roof of the cottage,
The boat pulled up on dry
Land, a curving jetty.
Off to the side, another
Sow awaiting her bloody
Demise. Because of the background
Of a dense web of hatching,
The main action takes place
In utmost gloom. You can see
Where a table has been removed.
A stenographic broken
Line allows light to diffuse
Through the tumbled interior of the cottage.
The pine behind it looms
Like a pyramid of angels,
Stacked up and trying to fly.
A sleeping old man near a fire-pit
With his hand snugged in his vest
Is either a philosopher
Or a personification of sloth.
The artist seems to intend him
As a counterpart to his
(The artist's) mother, depicted
Opposite. There is a certain
Fondness for vulgar subjects:

The goddess is scored in painful
Realism; a dog
Is casually cleaning himself
As Joseph dreams. Devotion
To the sky is unusual. Confusion
Overwhelms the shepherds and their flock,
Possibly because they have seen
The squatting woman, illuminated
From behind, urinating
And defecating, though looking
Over her shoulder to make sure
They are not watching.
Despondency
And cheerfulness contend,
As do astonishment
And indignation.
Actually, of course,
The whole world is watching.

Much of the language for this poem was suggested by a, perhaps badly
translated, museum brochure.

# Nike

In protest against atrocity
Airplanes full of people flew

Into the symbolic buildings,
Also full of people.

Things flew out of the buildings,
For example a sneaker with a foot still in it.

Imagine the Mastermind's surprise—
I mean *all* the way down?

In protest against atrocity,
This girl I know threw a bucket

Of scarlet paint against a stucco wall.
When the random splash and run

Assumed the shape of a tree, perfectly,
Blood-Weeping Willow,

Imagine the Mastermind's surprise:
It wasn't supposed to be beautiful, just true.

In protest against atrocity,
I fell in love with a beautiful girl.

Want to know what it feels like?
Quiet.

The first time, as a child,
The Mastermind saw rain

He was very quiet.
He'd never seen rain before,

But no one had to tell him what it was
Because, he was, you know…

That's how quiet I was
The first time I saw her,

The way her hair swept and swayed
In breeze, every breath she breathed,

In protest against atrocity.
She had to be careful not to smile,

Because she was so beautiful
Her smiling led to widespread swooning,

Falling buildings.
She held a black belt in smiling.

I was like a child seeing rain,
Or a falling building,

For the first time.
In protest against atrocity

The leaves discussed their lives
In the systole and the diastole of breezes.

But now it is quiet.
The kind of quiet nothing enters

And nothing issues from.
No Mastermind.

Quiet as a bullet
In a revolver's chamber

Under the mattress
In the house

In the meaningless little village.
Quiet as the word *explosion*

On page three hundred
Of a closed, shelved, and musty novel,

An unrecognized masterpiece.
Shh.

Quiet as dust,
As the dusting of snow

Covering someone you know.
Quiet as the future. Trust me. That quiet.

Shh.
The future overflows with clemency.

# The Mastermind Asks Some Questions

Q. What is the nature of your presentation?

A. I always leave before the music starts.

Q. Why should obscene transgressions, then, occur?

A. The wind, it seems, is taking me personally.

Q. Do you know nothing of the art of being

Interrupted?

                 A. Yes. I want to feel

Lucky, and be someone else's luck.

Q. Do you think your teeth are under the fallen building?

A. Why else would I keep digging for them there?

Q. Are you seeking closure for your teeth?

A. Every closure is an aperture.

Q. Whatever will you do if you should find them?

A. Give them to the loved ones, the lucky ones.

Q. Survivors of the victims, who need closure?

A. Yes. Them. All of them. All of us. Us.

Q. What about me?

                 A. You? What about you?

# A Fable

Early morning,
After the bitch had whelped
A litter of mutts,
The son dressed for school.

The old man presented him
With a black plastic bag—
Twelve drowned pups,
A sack of bastards—
And said,
*Find you a ditch*
*On your way to school*
*And throw 'em in.*
What, besides what
He was told,
Was there to do?

The old man lost
A front tooth
Where a horse kicked him
And then his whole left side—
Paralyzed from a stroke.
He had to limp around,
But he could limp around.

When the old man wanted
Another drink
He just lifted his glass skyward
And yelled his daughter's name,
Said, *Three fingers.*
(There was no mother,
Nor had there ever been.)
When the old man wanted

More spring water
To mix with his rum,
He rattled the dipper
In the steel pail
And yelled the name of his son.

One day
The old man sat drinking
The afternoon away
On his front porch.
He said to his son,
*That spruce tree has grown.*
*It's starting to block my view*
*Of the high country.*
*I want you to cut it down.*
The son just turned
And walked away.

The old man died
And, then, so did the tree.
They put the old man in the dirt,
Unceremoniously.
The tree, well,
The son cut it down
And bucked it up
For firewood.
When he was done he said,
*There. How do you like your view*
*Of the high country?*

# Stop Whimpering and Speak

Sad Master, I see you coming from very far
Away, leading your bony, wind-broke horse.
Turn back. I'm busy dividing my time.
My love is the death of kisses. I live
With her apart in the wind of constancy.
There's nothing you can do, given what you have done.

# Members of the Board

As usual, the Go-to Guy was gone.
No one knew where. Actually he was
Saving, from a burning building, a box
Of matches which he immediately rushed
To the Unbelievable Match Museum.

The boardroom was evacuated but
For the Mastermind's voice on the speakerphone.
"Listen carefully," drooled the black box.
"For those of you who have a friend in Jesus,
So long. Enjoy the Eternal Board Meeting.

Think fondly of those of us still funning in Hell,
Who loved the world too much and were, admit it,
Much more interesting than you were."
All along the Wiseguy guarded the door
To the boardroom he didn't know was empty.

No one ever got past him. If they tried
He shot off all their noses, which stopped them cold.
The Expert had gone home to try something.
This time it was rubber bands, his testicles,
Drinking bleach, and blowtorching his face.

Every time he heard, "Don't try this at home,
Boys and girls," he went right home and tried it.
After all, he was the Expert, right?
Meanwhile, the Idea Guy had just
Written a sonnet that could save the ozone

Layer. He tried to get through to the Mastermind.
He tried and tried and tried and tried and tried.

# The Music

No one hears the conductor of the music, and only a pathological optimism allows us even to hear the music as such—instead of math—interval, duration, mechanism, or just plain noise.

We live within a prison—I mean prism—where all we recognize are some reflections—I mean refractions—all the busted colors of what we've done.

Trying to forget all that, I drive my music box right down the middle of the prism.

My music box has no conductor.

Only me and "Für Elise."

I had some competition from a tiny thumping low-ride pickup, and also from an ice-cream truck pursued by a lazy tornado of toddlers.

I kept my eye on them in the mirror.

After that it was just me and Elise on cruise, conductorless.

My music box don't handle so good but she always sounds like angels, my music box.

# When She Sings

There's a flight of birds furling and glancing
Over the city as the wineglass musician
(Is there a word for that?)
Sets up his folding table and tunes his crystal chalices
(A little more, a little less)
On Via Giulia.
He lays his hat on the pavement,
But he doesn't look destitute.
He smiles openly but his eyes are sad
(A little more, a little less).
I think he likes the way "Für Elise" sounds
When played on chalices.
He fingers a sponge of vinegar between phrases
To keep the music dulcet, pure,
As if each glass were an angel
Whose voice he touches to ring.
The birds stream over. They disappear and reappear
By banking, like a black streamer of smoke or Mylar
Over the Eternal City.
Suddenly the wineglass musician stops, midphrase
And looks up at the birds.
That's how I know. That's how I know
That on the far side of town,
In a small room in Villa Chiaraviglio,
She must be singing
To herself as she arranges the zinnias,
An American tune, in her crystalline voice,
A hymn about how
It's the end of the world and life goes on.

# Orbit Obit

From this far out in orbit, everything
Is infinitesimal, and very clear,
Like the little trigger part of your ear
With a wisp of blond slacked behind it.

From this far out in orbit, nothing
Is big or vague, like church, but the line in the sand
Keeps moving. From this far out in orbit your eyes
Are quatrocento islands of towers all

Atilt, where all the women go blind from making lace,
And all the men are fishermen who mend
Their nets each sunset, and sooner or later are lost at sea.
From this far out the Hemlock Society

Writes me a letter in which they offer to help
Me kill myself for a small contribution.
The line in the sand has passed me by.
From this far out in orbit the tip of your tongue,

The white hush of your hip, your palm proffered to be licked,
The event horizon of your lower lip,
All good places to start and end,
Since no one ever mentioned going home.

# A Cast of Thousands

Want some violence? I thought so.
A young buck jumped the barbed-wire fence
But misstepped and caught a hind leg
In the twist of top wire and next-
To-top wire. He hung head down and fought.
You can imagine the rest. Just try.
The slow death, the opacity of eyes.
How long do you think it took? Guess.
Terror that flailed the grass down to dirt,
That scraped the dirt down to rock and kept scraping
Before the sacred shock set in,
Hypothermia, the last heart-thud.
That spring I found the emptied carcass
Hanging. I was fixing fence.
By then the violence was gone.
It was just a skeleton with ribbons
Of hide lifting in the breeze.
On the ground a mound of fur where
Red ants were busy living.

# Canto V (*Inf.*) Revisited (I-80 West)

The day that love exiled me from life,
The interstate was a spinning wheel of wind.
A blizzard of cornhusks took away the sky (*smarrito*),
And made the roadside fences trellises
Of dead foliage.
Semis listed along, massively sleepy,
Until they tipped over,
And lay still.
The meek turned on their lights.

I missed my adversary,
And noticed a sense of nostalgic intimacy,
As I fingered the scars he gave me.
I tried to think of my friends from the city
For whom nature is something you sneak up on
And identify.
I love them for that.
I tried to invoke my interest
In the undesirable body types

That dominate the sidewalks of our cities,
How people compel me almost as much
As ships or possums, but not as much as clouds.
"The avant-garde is lost in exposition,"
I intoned. It didn't help. I asked,
"Where did all this death come from?" Nothing.
As I glided into Wyoming,
Droves of tumbleweeds roiled toward me,
Completely ravishing the road ahead.

I forgave my love, in advance, for leaving me,
Since, let's face it, there's not that much of me
Left to leave.

But then, there I was again,
Thinking of her,
My sail.

# Child's Play

Eeny, meeny,
Cross my heart.
Please.
Stick a needle in
A haystack
Made of money.
I don't mind.
Just don't blink.
Die. Or hope to.
Just don't blink.
Years made of money
And hot air
Ballooned over us.
After the drought
The river took
Back everything.

# Two Sketches of Horses

As for the three horses
Standing under the tree when
Lightning hit it,
One was old,
The horse I rode as a kid.
One was a colt I was starting.
One was beautiful, a gunmetal
Blue roan, and way too crazy to ride.
One by one I put
A rope around their necks
And dragged them behind the truck
To a low spot, where scavengers
Could do their work in peace.
The crazy one—that was
The first time she'd had
A rope around her neck.
I went back a year later.
Coyotes hadn't scattered their bones,
But the three skeletons were clean
So it was like
Three horses running together,
White ghost horses running
Lying down across the
Surface of the earth.

*

Tonight a beautiful girl,
Blond hair loose about her shoulders,
Walks out into the pasture
With a bag of carrots.
The wildflowers printed on
Her summer dress match
(Or close enough)

The real wildflowers in the field.
The butterflies stitched
On her cowboy boots
Match the butterflies
That rise where she walks
And settle back into the tall grass
Where she passes.
Six yearling colts come up
To nuzzle her and get their carrots.
Beyond her, snowy mountains
And the sunset detonating
A tree-shaped cloud.
I watch from the doorway,
And for a minute, maybe longer,
Everything
That threatens us
Threatens to save us.

# Unentitled

My love told me she owned the waterfall, the one that we had climbed so far to see.

             How could I not but believe her claim?

                            So I
asked her, "What does it entail in terms of upkeep, nourishment, health care, and possibly the emotional well-being of a being so free-flowing, so fell, and ungraspable as waterfalls are known to be?"

All she said was, "I'm not the only one.

                   You own it, too."

                      Think
about the girl you love.

          Does she love you?

               Love you like a
waterfall?

      If she doesn't, wait for one who does.

# What Do You Want to Be When You Grow Up?

It's not as though the president can't feel
Nostalgia for the days
When bombers were like bumblebees,
And a single chubby bad boy could flash
One hundred thirty-seven thousand souls
Into the afterlife.
But progress is a one-way street, pal,
And the new, black, titanium manta rays
Look more sinister and shifty.

A black titanium manta ray slips
Under radar, skims the storm,
The jungle canopy, and roofs of a jigsawed town.
It flies so low the pilot sees
The O-shaped mouths and covered ears
Of survivors, who are busy mopping up
After the wave that came over them
From out of geological time.

The world knows we are a generous people.

The first we saw of the wave,
It was a drunken tongue, swollen beyond words,
Relaxed, yet cadaverous,
A slush of buses, huts, huts' inhabitants, rolled boats,
Paint-flecked boards, and rusty nails.
What was not borne on the wave, I ask you?
Still, the footage hurt.
The footage had a tag on its big toe.

The manta flies at night, invisible,
Across the innocent sea.

Startled awake, you open your eyes in the dark.
The manta ray flies into your open eyes.
Close them. Good. You are the President.

## As Is

When she sleeps
She must be in Senegal somewhere.
The tide goes out from every shore
In the world,
And in the middle of the sea
A mountain made of water
Holds its breath.

When she sleeps
Everything depends
On all the wheel barrows
Except the red one.
Ordinary women
Bump into walls,
And Shakespeare writes
One more sonnet
None of us will ever read.

When she sleeps
The automobiles of the elderly
Drift to the shoulder
Out of respect.
Ducks tuck heads under wings,
And pelicans can't make water landings.
They flip like confetti in wind.

When she sleeps
The moon hums,
Unable to rise or fall.
A green kite with a broken string
Thrashes in bare branches.
I stay awake to make sure she sleeps
(I never trusted that wheel
Barrow).

When she sleeps
I believe
I believe
I believe
I'll never break these chains.

Don't wake up, babe.
You're just too beautiful as is.

# The Decisive Moment

*A photograph is death at work*
RICHARD HUGO

There's a 1956 photo by Cartier-Bresson
Of a skinny Italian girl
In a white blouse and plaid skirt,
Skipping over the bridge that spans
The canal on the island
Of Torcello.
Tamarisk thrives along the dead canal.
There are no children now
On the island of Torcello,
Population twelve, all pensioners.
And the bridge over the canal
Is mossy from no one crossing.
Did she ever have children?
Did she leave for America?
Did she have her mother's Bedouin eyes,
Her father's crush on the sea?
The farmhouse she grew up in
Is a ruin now, its fields fallow,
Its roof in the kitchen,
Her bedroom likewise fallen.
School is out, and home is just
Over the bridge.
The girl appears to be
Lifting off out of the picture.
She's happy going home,
Out of school.
She's almost over the bridge,
Almost out of the frame, airborne.
That girl is my age now,

If she is still alive,
My tamarisk.

# My Sister

My sister is a place where
Sorrel horses walk single file through tall
Lodgepole stands,
Where sunlight severs down and dulls and shatters
Before it hits the ground,
Where the grass is tall saw grass, wavy
Like the grass in the Sargasso Sea,
Where eels spawn and the new eels
Migrate to the continents of their parents'
Origin, inexplicably...
We don't know how they do that.
Life is nothing if not obvious.

My sister is a place where
I left the gas cap on top of the '82 Land Cruiser.
It's got to be around here somewhere,
But I can't find it,
And if it's around here
It's walled by snowy mountains where
The wildflowers (lupines, columbines, penstemon)
Bloom a month later than here,
And are smaller,
And all around are aspen trees turning yellow
As their yellow leaves turn in the wind,
Where things that fall and roll away
Cannot be found under the fragrant sage,
And as I look around, I'm thinking
Of the time I chained and churned and shoveled
That rig through five miles of thigh-deep snow,
Occasionally jacking it up in back
And tipping it off forward to keep going
Just to get to a phone to call a girl,
And the time I drove with my daughter

Across Nebraska and Iowa in 105 degrees,
Blocks of ice to cool us pooling on the floor.

My sister is a place where
Rivers swell in spring and falter in the fall.
My sister is a place
Where no time passes.
We cannot live there.

# Prayer

O beginning, daughters of the earth await the sons of heaven, and
vice versa.
    They all practice trigger-happiness and chicken scratch.

They practice duration and meltdown.
       They primp in your glass.

You think that's funny?
    Never mind.
      It's getting really cold in
here.
  Who makes the introductions if not you?
        Who initiates the
bliss? I ask.
   Have I not left footprints in hell?
        Mind-out-of-time, I
remain a false apology.
    There.
   All better now?
      You gave me a
body so I could learn to live without it, right?
       This poem is just a
way of minding my own business.
     It flourishes in your darkness.

This poem is not what you think.
     It's what thinks you.
       It thinks the
only hope we have, bombarding us with zeros, sending us our
mail-order teeth.
    Initiate the bliss, O ending.
      Take whatever you
want, and don't forget to close the door.

# World News

The Know-It-All could not believe his luck.
The Cut-Purse missed his chance and got the Willies.
Don't smirk. Iffy at best, the Dare Devil
Wasn't up to daring the real Devil,
Whose disappointment in the Cut-Purse was
Immense. He didn't know about the Know-
It-All. Oh what a bloody fool. Jesus.
The Know-It-All could not believe his luck,
And he was right, since everybody dies.
And being lucky in this life, God knows,
Is all or nothing. Ask the Know-It-All.
Or ask the Devil, if you want the truth.

# Cahoots

In the assembly of suicides
There is self-help, group therapy,
And a lot of waiting.

Black aspen leaves on a red, red road.
In the restaurant the white-jacketed waiters
Are really just waiting.

The guitarist has clearly been hired
To keep the restaurant empty.
What's taking us?

My character has no content.
The present lasts so long,
There's no need for a future.

Trapped inside a jiffy,
Let's get real.
People in Hell don't rot.

# Two Angels

There's something about Neil's brain—
I don't know what exactly—
Autism, Fetal Alcohol
Syndrome—that makes him different
From you, Reader, and
From me. Talking to Neil
Is like talking to a hearth fire.
Unlike us he'll never
Hurt anyone. There are
Angels among us, and we pity them.
Neil must be fourteen.
He's always vaguely smiling.
What he does is walk
His dog, August, who must
Also be fourteen—
A long-suffering Beagle.
August doesn't want to walk anymore.
But walking August is all
That Neil does. So August
Walks on doggedly.
August has arthritic
Andiron Beagle legs,
And rheumy glacial eyes.
From the front he resembles
An uncomfortable claw-foot wing chair.
His muzzle is like frost
On a hammer.
His gaze reminds me of
Bernini's Aeneas
Bearing his bitter father
Out of the burning city.
August doesn't have
A whole lot of miles left.

The first time I saw them
I was walking my dog.
I crossed the street to say
Hello. This is what
It's like to talk to Neil.
—Hi there.
—Hello (a little slurry).
What's your dog's name?
—His name is Dante.
—I didn't know that.
—What's your dog's name?
—August.
—Really? That's my middle name.
—I didn't know that (his
Perpetual smile broadens).
—And you. What's your name?
—My name is Neil.
—That's a nice name.
—See you.
And off they go on their
Never-ending round.
I wonder what Neil will do
When August gives out, which soon
He must, and leaves an endless
Absence in Neil's mind.
How will Neil go on
Without August? What will he do?
Oh, sit on the stoop and smile,
Remembering August, as if
It were today, yawn
And stretch his wings in the sun.

## Aptest Eve

Young man sweatsoaked in an iron bunk,
Death row, barracks, or monastery, does it matter?
Milksop hands of a pianist
Twisting and twisting the corner of a sheet,
Since lacking the white throat of a Chopin sonata.
Don't we all need something to do with our hands?
No. No we don't.

# Apollinaire's Cane

*for Dean Young*

The Mastermind was for a time
In possession of Apollinaire's ivory cane,
Carved from a narwhal tusk.
It was given to the Mastermind
By a famous lady philanthropist in Venice.
Apollinaire had forgotten his cane
On the philanthropist's dock,
His attention focused on stepping,
Drunk, into a gondola.
Apollinaire never missed his cane.
To him it was just a cane,
But for the Mastermind
It was the ivory cane of Apollinaire,
His most prized possession.
The Mastermind brought the cane
To Paris,
When he entered the Sorbonne
At the age of ten.
He took it everywhere,
And when people asked, "Why the cane?"
The Mastermind replied,
"It was Apollinaire's."
Did I mention the Mastermind was absentminded?
He forgot the famous cane
On the seat of a Parisian taxi.
As the taxi drove off, he remembered it.
He shouted and waved
But the cabbie didn't notice him.
The Mastermind watched as the cab disappeared
Into Paris,

And Apollinaire's cane
Ceased to be
Apollinaire's cane.

*

The salt was on the shelf
Next to the bottled ship.
Reaching for the salt one day,
The Mastermind hit the ship with his elbow.
The bottle broke, but the ship was fine.
Fine? What good is a tiny ship
Without a bottle to sail in?
It's not like it wanted to be free,
Sail a tiny sea,
Float in a bathtub with a child.
The point of a ship in a bottle
Is the bottle.
Apollinaire's cane never wanted
To be free of Apollinaire, either.
Apollinaire's cane
Is not Apollinaire's cane.
The ship without the bottle
Will never be the same.
Don't touch me.

# Girl without Her Nightgown

The dance was slow, was slow, was slow.
Slow was the dance, very.
The dancer turned, her arms held out
As she came closer, slowly.

Wood grain steams in morning light, Mama,
The hulls of boats asunder.
Sterns still sport their stupid names.
The dance was slow, was slow, was slow.
Slow was the dance, very.

Scratch and snitch is the raven's game.
He nods and gossips.
Have you ever seen such happy rats?
What puppies.
The dance was slow, was slow, was slow.
Slow was the dance, very.

Those overturned boats are sepulchers of air.
All the boats that aren't washed up
Prowl the flooded streets, poke corpses with oars.
The water is on fire.
The dance was slow, was slow, was slow.
Slow was the dance, very.

Slow dance on the water, Mama.
I have a sack slung over my shoulder. Loot.
It's like I'm stealing my own soul.
The dance is slow, Mama.
I don't know where you are.

# In My Daughter's Room

Our house-shaped spacecraft spiraled earthward.
I felt like Dorothy.
Just after reentry
The loudmouth member of the crew
Ganked the only parachute and Geronimo'd,
Leaving us two
Tailspinning. Irony was
The parachute was not a parachute,
But one of those weather balloons you never
See anymore,
That used to bob in the stratosphere
Like tinfoil diadems,

Never getting anywhere,
But with a great ocean-view,
Until finally something gives
And a farmer finds it
Strewn across his hog-lot.
The house-craft touched down
Safely in a bed of flame.
The farthest away
I've ever been
Is inside my own home.
My daughter's room.
Today.

I think black holes are just plastic
Garbage bags blowing down the midnight highway
That is the Universe.
There aren't as many dimensions as we thought.
A black hole can disappear anything that nears it.
We all know that.
The farthest away I've ever been is in my own home,
Finally cleaning out my daughter's room

So another little girl can live here.
The black plastic bag I held in my hand
Was infinitely capacious.
I mean I could throw anything in there.

It was a black hole,
The Universe's way of cleaning up.
Just to prove its ability,
I threw in a horse.
Not a toy horse, a real one
Named Too Cute to Shoot, a dressage champion.
Then, for good measure, I threw in another horse.
This one was Whiskey River, the best ranch horse ever.
Then I threw in the sun.
Then a pair of angel wings
And a magic wand
That was supposed to bring

Good luck.
It's junk.
All the small clothes are in the attic,
Should anyone ever have another daughter.
I threw away a notebook that was blank
Except for the first page
That had the beginning of a Shakespeare sonnet:
Let me not to the marriage of true minds / Admit.
The whole poem is writ
In lipstick on the window,
And though I could have, I didn't throw
Away any windows. I threw away the satin pillow

That bore a golden ring up the stairway to the castle,
Some old Cosmos. The cosmos.
The jaws of life. The passage of time,
The eternal present.
I threw away a year in Italy.

Sixteen summers in Wyoming. The garden.
A porcelain unicorn. Then I was done.
I stood in the middle of my daughter's swirling room,
The black bag in one hand,
And in the other a small glass horse from Murano,
A piece of tourist kitsch,
Which I kept, and keep.

# The Swamp:

Swamp life depends on rot,
Like all life, but more so.
Swamp folk say,
*Don't go in there,* and they should know.
Everything is hidden, poisonous, and tricky.
For instance:

Swamp swans.
Swamps are necessary and feature swans,
Bowed, bowed, heartless, and Pre-
Raphaelite, like a corporation:

What people don't know:
Swans stink,
Like swamps, only worse;
Like exhaust from a Greyhound bus, with a
Hint of fetid lilac.

Under their flinty feathers,
Little towns, metropoli, highways, fortified
Walls, busy fields,
Whole empires of parasites.

What everyone knows about alligators:
Doctors pretending to be rotten logs.

They lead the unexamined life.
Once, as I stepped over a rotten log deep
Within the swamp,
A cottonmouth opened its cotton mouth and
Reared up,
Fearless as an exclamation mark, and
Making a sound like cotton:
The primordial swamp word for thirst.

Then he sashay-swam away.
What people don't know:
How lucky they are,
Cottonmouths, I mean.

A swamp is steadfast:
Death in death and death in death.
What's in the swamp stays in the swamp.
A swamp is a terrible tragedy.
It stinks in the literary as well as in
The literal sense.
Because
Without a messenger, there's just, you know,
The message:

# Treasure Island

I felt like I was sending the wrong signal
From the lighthouse.
Amnesiac waves swashbuckled in
From where pirates keelhauled the ne'er-do-well.
As usual, I was the last to know.

In the city by the sea were tall, shiny buildings
From which the sea could be looked down on.
A hush fell in the boardroom
Like a truckload of goose down.
Some board members thought they smelled elbow grease,

But that was impossible.
Then the Mastermind's voice on the speakerphone:
Exit the building. Say nothing to anyone.
They did. And they didn't.
The waves laid the ne'er-do-well gently

At the high-tide line.
The Mastermind donned his swashbuckle
And waited.
The tide receded, bowing and kneeling.
Everything went back to normal.

Just kidding.

# The Stagnation

The stagnation is deafening.
Then some menacing
Nudists walk past
Laughing, which doesn't
Affect the stagnation.
I hold out my hands,
Palms turned down,
And rain rains from them,
Which affects the stagnation
But not much.
Here come the nudists
Again, wielding
Tire irons and saps.
The wind kicks up,
Affecting the stagnation.
The rotary clothesline
Starts spinning to beat hell,
Clothes like garish,
Terrified clowns—
Did you ever notice
How easy it is
To terrify clowns?
They're already crying
Before the fun
Begins—clowns
Clinging to the rotors
Of a Navy helicopter
Whose fuselage
Is camouflage—
The desert kind—
Whose rocket
Launchers are loaded,

Whose orders are
Anybody's guess.

# Our Clandestiny

As it fell out in the end the only thing
Wrong with dreaming was it was too much
Like being awake. Secure the perimeter.

Out there in the early dark the watchers
Are watching us. The coughers are coughing,
Politely waiting for the waiters. I dreamed

I loaded my driveway into the trunk of your car,
And we escaped. The smokers were smoking
And occasionally coughing and, as always,

Watching the waiters. The perimeter
Cannot be secured. The death toll never
Falls. All the beggars are taking riding lessons.

The background is going by them way too fast.
Dante's narcolepsy made God's hair
Stand on end, but at the end of three days,

The Master Dream was all there was anyway.
There were flying colors, then up rose
The jerkwater moon, the shepherd moon, which led

Us two away into this silver pasture.

# Life Eliminates Art

She wrote a poem about a man in flames.
Next day a real man in flames was on
The news all day. He flamed into the airport
At Glasgow, then (get this) he tried to run.
Seems he was some sort of doctor trying
To do no harm. Hmm. Harm to whom?
He had to be extinguished by authorities.
No one noticed the coincidence,
But the realm is forced to rethink Wimbledon.
My guess—the boink-ka-boink must (must!) go on.

She wrote a poem about a farrier
Whose ribs were cracked while trying to shoe a colt.
Next day the local paper featured
A stove-in farrier and an unshod pony.
Ouch. But no one took much notice of this
Coincidence. How farriers fare—who cares?

She wrote a poem in which a gang of neighbors
Came over to kill me. I'm writing as fast as I can
'Cause here they come, mostly armed with ax
Handles and chains. No one will take note
That there's a pattern here. It's very clear,
But she won't ever write the poem where
Someone really gets it.

# Trying to Live These Days

Needless to say,
The naysayer and the do-gooder
Are one and the same.
The new moon chases the sun.
The full moon faces it down.

I'm talking to you, scamperwit,
With that teardrop on your breast.
I'm trying to drive a nail underwater
Into the hull of the treasure ship.
Needless to say,

I hope I'm wrong about everything
Because if I'm right we're fucked.
Like you could throw a cold woodstove into reverse
And vacuum down a shard of cloud,
And a tiny quadrant of sky,

Then another cloud chip,
Then another sky piece,
Until four bluebirds hang head down,
Stuck in the flue.
We always make an icon of our fear.

The one we found hanging from its broken beak
Jammed in the twisted strand
Of barbed wire,
Beak right under the barb.
The pair that plagued my chimney

With cradle building
Four years running.
We always make an icon of our fear.

I hope the spring doesn't run dry—
Another dry run of when you say goodbye.

I think I'll fall through the floor again.
I think I'll fall head down down a mine shaft or a well.
Bluebirds mean spring. That's what they sing.
"A quiet warbling dawn song" (Audubon).
When I ripped their prairie-grass nest

Out of the chimney top,
They didn't say a thing.
When I spilled their brood on the ground,
They said nothing.
Things go wrong while trying to live these days.

The new moon chases the sun.
The full moon faces it down.

# My Father's Three Kindnesses

My father thought nothing
Of putting his children
On rank horses.
He thought it was good for us.
We did child-breaking
Research on ground.

Also he thought nothing
Of leaving us alone
For days, even weeks,
At a time. He thought
That was good for us, too.
We, my sisters
And I, are no
Strangers to loneliness.

But he did, in his life,
Three kind things
That I should say.
He sewed each of us
A doeskin bag
That held a pocketknife,
Matches, a fishhook and line,
A snare, and a whistle
For when we got lost.

Also, I remember
One morning, deer hunting.
I was twelve.
A wet snow had come
The night before.
My feet were soaked
And the sun wasn't up.

My teeth were like
A sewing machine.

He built a small fire
There on the side hill
In the deep woods.
He got wet twigs
To burn by feathering them
Out with his knife.

Then as I started
To feel the warmth
He pulled two
Bacon sandwiches
From his pocket
And gave me one.

# The Suffering Shades Were in the Ice
## (*Inf.* XXXII)

> ...*vidi due sì stretti*
> *che 'l pel del capo avìeno insieme misto.*

Remember when we were dead together?
Those were the days.
A mirror fell from the sky and didn't break,
But we were still afraid to walk on it.
We thought it might break us.
Then you were crying in my arms
But you weren't even here.
You were in a different hemisphere,
Being an otter, loving fun.
A kind woman is just as rare
(This should surprise you) as a kind man.

Remember when the sun abandoned our planets?
For a while the Southern Hemisphere was okay.
But then it wasn't. Darkness fell.
Let me know when darkness rises.
Strangely life wasn't any more lonely
Than previously. Yes, I'm sure.
Remember when the rank and file looked up?
That was unnerving.

# The Red Telephone

I heard the distinct
Sound

Of whimpering and weeping.
It seemed

To be coming from
The telephone,

Which was on
The hook.

When I picked up
The receiver,

It was like a fistful
Of nettles.

Hello? I said.
Hello?

Who is this?
Nothing.

Whimpering. Weeping.
Then I

Realized there was no one
On the other

End. The telephone
Was crying.

I took it from my ear
And looked at it.

What's wrong? I asked.
You can tell me.

It felt like a fistful
Of nettles

In my hand, but there was no
Answer.

Just the weeping and whimpering
Of the telephone.

# A Red Flag (On the Smallness of Her Hands and Feet)

*nobody, not even Loraine, has such*
*small hands*

DORA

I'm not myself today, alas.
Her hands are nanohands.
Her feet are nano, too.
But she takes all bulls by the horns
And teases bunnies out of their hats.
(Bunnies have nanohats, in case you didn't know.)

Just because she's out of earshot, sight,
Across the sea I cannot even see from here
Doesn't mean she's out of heartshot, does it?
Or does it? Take these snapshots that she sent.
See the nanohands and -feet? She's fair
And happy. Does she miss me insufficiently?

Nanotechnology has not reached the heart as yet,
But it's on its way, trust me.
Her heart across the sea, her sweet loneliness—
I mean loveliness—is killing me—out of sight and earshot.
Heartshot is what I am. I'm not myself today, alas,
Remembering the small touch of her hands,

As if the moon had breathed on me.

## No Bastion

I had a tree house, like every boy, but I didn't build mine in the
woods, the way other boys do, or in backyards.

                            I chose, instead, an
old limber pine that clenched a granite outcrop on the open prairie.

My tree was old, but low to the ground, wind-crippled, a bastion
of nothing.

              Yes, I had secrets, but they were safe in my wastrel
tree, adrift beneath my reeling sky.

                        And from its low heights I
could see a hundred miles across the prairie, and all the way to the
snowy bite of high country.

               I wasn't atavistic.

                        I just wanted to see
all the way.

             My tree house was more of a base, nesty thing, where
I could be up in the sky and close to the ground.

                     It was just a
platform of sawmill slabs and the backseat of a '48 jeep.

                        And I had
my binoculars.

             At any given time I could see six or seven bands of
antelope salted across the distances, and redtails above, turning the
wheels of the world.

             Sometimes I'd slink down to see how close I
could get to those radar-sighted antelope, figuring contours of
sage-dizzy draws and fishy breezes, staying out of sight, staying
downwind.

             Once, I lay out in the sage and grass, undetected by a
small herd maybe fifty yards off, when a coyote, playing the same
game as me, coming up the wind, stepped over me as if I were a
log.

I had seen him coming, knew he hadn't seen me, and when he

spooked, the pronghorns bolted into the distance, looking for a deeper emptiness to hide in.

I was happy and went back to my tree.

I stayed until the stars began to whirl.

I was hidden, but easy to find, had anyone wanted to find me.

# Blue or Green

We don't belong to each other.
               We belong together.
                              Some poems
belong together to prove the intentionality of subatomic particles.

Some poems eat with scissors.
                    Some poems are like kissing a
porcupine.
          God, by the way, is disappointed in some of your recent
choices.
         Some poems swoop.
                      When she said my eyes were
definitely blue, I said, *How can you see that in the dark?*
                                        *How can*
*you not?* she said, and that was like some poems.
                                    Some poems are
blinded three times.
               Some poems go like death before dishonor.

Some poems go like the time she brought cherries to the movies;
later a heedless picnic in her bed.
                      Never revered I crumbs so
highly.
       Some poems have perfect posture, as if hanging by
filaments from the sky.
                 Those poems walk like dancers,
noiselessly.
          All poems are love poems.
                            Some poems are better off
dead.
     Right now I want something I don't believe in.

# When I Rest

When I rest my head over her heart,
I can hear the rowing,
Paddle-splash and oarlock-knock;
I can feel the pull
Into the swiftest run.
I can hear the current's pleas for silence,
*This is important,*
The better to hear her heart.
I feel like a blue feather in her skiff.
The river loves the sea, which absently
Brushes its hair, waiting,
Unconcerned by the separations of lovers
It causes.
The sea has tides.
The tides have swells.
The swells have waves
From so much brushing.
When we glide asea, it's sunset so
We get to watch the river become the rose.

## *Freud* Spelled Backwards

Itsy-bitsy,
You're killing me
In the best possible way.
The lighthouse,
Our hope,
Blinks,
"Keep away
Or sink."
I'm a wreck.
And what is sex
*Not* about?
Your boat
Is watertight.
Who baked the Forbidden Cookies,
My trilobite?
In hindsight
Any dumb gumshoe could decipher
That the end
Began
In the foyer
Where you dropped your
Keys
On the floor.
Then there was
The rumpled rug,
Your cowboy boots asplay,
The trail of lingerie
Leading up to… after-play.
Atrociously fragile odalisque,
Amazed, amazing, lit,
Wake me even
If I'm dreaming

Of you. The only risk
Is in not taking it.

# Still and All

A moist spring evening lowers itself
Onto the fragrance of lilacs and cherry blossoms,
Like the sadness you wish would last a little longer.

These days we do it every time
Someone drops a hat.
Sometimes we do it even

When no one drops a hat.
It should always be like that,
Don't you think?

In Iraq right now, someone's doing it, no?
They have to. Despite everything.
And one of these days one of these days

Will be just one of these days.

# The Fall Guy

Hello?
Is this The Fall Guy?
Speaking.
Did you take the fall?
It's what I do.
So, you're in prison now?
You call it prison. Prison is my heaven,
My afterlife.

# All That I Can Tell from Here

I live in a town of no cross streets,
Just serpentines and stairs.
That's how steep it is above the bay.
So there's
A house across the ravine it would take
Twenty minutes to reach,
But to look at—
It's a hundred yards away.
They
Have a sunroom with north-facing windows,
These neighbors I don't know.
The house needs paint,
So they've hired a guy
Who works to a boom box.
He paints in time.
Hip-hop? Opera?
I can't hear it.
Between the clapboard and trim,
He conducts the paint onto wood.
Should
I care about the painter's taste in music?
Up and down, side to side,
Andante.
His left hand wavers for balance
Since
He's poised on the top
Of a step
Ladder,
The step that says,
THIS IS NOT A STEP,
Pointing out the obvious,
A technicality.
Then I halfway see,

66

In the sunroom,
Someone
Dancing, or so it seems—
Chassé?
I can't see.
Andante.
And farther back in the shadows
Of the sunroom—
The partner?
Carried along
By the same song?
Then I think they are not dancing
At all.
Are *they* painting, too?
An action
Collaboration
On a large canvas?
The only thing
They can't be doing
Is composing
A poem.
That would be
Me,
All hunched over and spying.
Now I see.
It's a music lesson.
I'm almost certain.
The teacher conducts,
Instructs,
Sways in time,
Charmed.
The violin swoons
In the student's arms.
But I can't be certain
Till the painter calls it a day,

And the student descends the stairs
With what appears
To be a violin case,
Which one can only assume
Contains a violin.
All this to arrive at the obvious:
Life is not a technicality,
So art can't be.
And that, my darling, is all
That I can tell
From here.


Wellington, NZ

## ABOUT THE AUTHOR

James Galvin was raised in northern Colorado. He has published six previous collections of poetry, most recently *X* (Copper Canyon Press, 2003). He is also the author of the critically acclaimed prose book *The Meadow* (Holt, 1992) and a novel, *Fencing the Sky* (Holt, 1999). His honors include a Lila Wallace – Reader's Digest Foundation Award, a Lannan Literary Award, and fellowships from the Guggenheim Foundation, the Ingram Merrill Foundation, and the National Endowment for the Arts. He has a home, some land, and some horses outside of Tie Siding, Wyoming, and he is a member of the permanent faculty of the University of Iowa Writers' Workshop.

# Lannan

## LANNAN LITERARY SELECTIONS

For two decades Lannan Foundation has supported the publication and distribution of exceptional literary works. Copper Canyon Press gratefully acknowledges their support.

LANNAN LITERARY SELECTIONS 2009

Michael Dickman, *The End of the West*
James Galvin, *As Is*
Heather McHugh, *Upgraded to Serious*
Lucia Perillo, *Inseminating the Elephant*
Connie Wanek, *On Speaking Terms*

RECENT LANNAN LITERARY SELECTIONS FROM
COPPER CANYON PRESS

Lars Gustafsson, *A Time in Xanadu,* translated by John Irons
David Huerta, *Before Saying Any of the Great Words: Selected Poems,* translated by Mark Schafer
June Jordan, *Directed by Desire: The Collected Poems*
Sarah Lindsay, *Twigs and Knucklebones*
W.S. Merwin, *Migration: New & Selected Poems*
Valzhyna Mort, *Factory of Tears,* translated by Franz Wright and Elizabeth Oehlkers Wright
Taha Muhammad Ali, *So What: New & Selected Poems, 1971–2005,* translated by Peter Cole, Yahya Hijazi, and Gabriel Levin
Dennis O'Driscoll, *Reality Check*
Kenneth Rexroth, *The Complete Poems of Kenneth Rexroth*
Ruth Stone, *In the Next Galaxy*
C.D. Wright, *One Big Self: An Investigation*
Matthew Zapruder, *The Pajamaist*

For a complete list of Lannan Literary Selections from Copper Canyon Press, please visit Partners on our Web site:
**www.coppercanyonpress.org**

The Chinese character for poetry is made up of two parts: "word" and "temple." It also serves as pressmark for Copper Canyon Press.

Since 1972, Copper Canyon Press has fostered the work of emerging, established, and world-renowned poets for an expanding audience. The Press thrives with the generous patronage of readers, writers, booksellers, librarians, teachers, students, and funders—everyone who shares the belief that poetry is vital to language and living.

Major funding has been provided by:

Anonymous

Beroz Ferrell & The Point, LLC

Cynthia Hartwig and Tom Booster

Lannan Foundation

National Endowment for the Arts

Cynthia Lovelace Sears and Frank Buxton

Washington State Arts Commission

*For information and catalogs:*
COPPER CANYON PRESS
Post Office Box 271
Port Townsend, Washington 98368
360-385-4925
www.coppercanyonpress.org

This book was designed and typeset by Phil Kovacevich. The text is set in Adobe Garamond, designed by Robert Slimbach for Adobe Systems, Inc. The headings are set in Sackers Gothic Medium. Printed on archival-quality paper at McNaughton & Gunn, Inc.